PEYTON MANNING

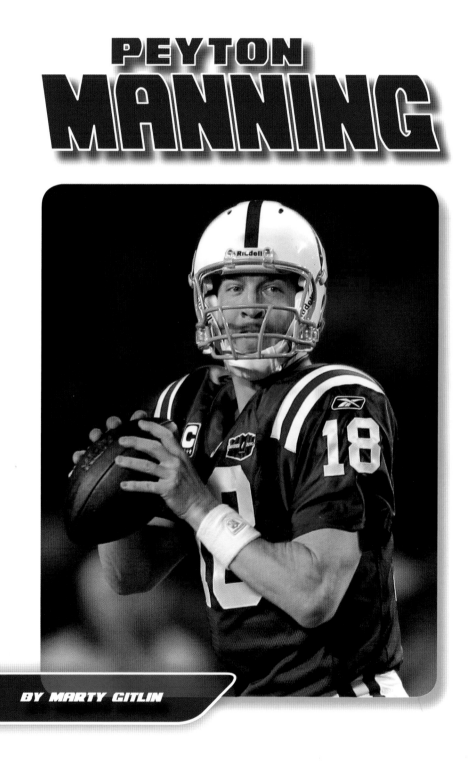

BY MARTY GITLIN

Published by ABDO Publishing Company, 8000 West 78th Street, Edina, Minnesota 55439. Copyright © 2011 by Abdo Consulting Group, Inc. International copyrights reserved in all countries. No part of this book may be reproduced in any form without written permission from the publisher. SportsZone™ is a trademark and logo of ABDO Publishing Company.

Printed in the United States of America,
North Mankato, Minnesota
112010
012011

Editor: Chrös McDougall
Copy Editor: Susan M. Freese
Interior Design and Production: Craig Hinton
Cover Design: Craig Hinton

Photo Credits: Matt Slocum/AP Images, cover; Paul Spinelli/AP Images, 4, 16, 25, 29; NFL Photos/AP Images, 7; Matt Stamey/AP Images, 8; Doug Mills/AP Images, 10; Mark Humphrey/AP Images, 13; Adam Nadel/AP Images, 14; Jeff Roberson/AP Images, 19; Tom Strickland/AP Images, 20; Greg Trott/AP Images, 22; Marco Garcia/AP Images, 26

Library of Congress Cataloging-in-Publication Data

Gitlin, Marty.
  Peyton Manning : superstar quarterback / by Marty Gitlin.
     p. cm. — (Playmakers)
  ISBN 978-1-61714-748-7
  1. Manning, Peyton—Juvenile literature. 2. Football players—United States—Biography—Juvenile literature. 3. Quarterbacks (Football)—United States—Biography—Juvenile literature. I. Title.
  GV939.M289G58 2011
  796.332092—dc22
  [B]
                                  2010046356

TABLE OF CONTENTS

CHAPTER 1

BORN INTO GRIDIRON GREATNESS

It was never going to be easy for Archie Manning's sons to match his athletic achievements. Archie was one of the top quarterbacks in the National Football League (NFL) during the 1970s. But his three sons certainly tried to match his greatness.

Peyton Manning was the second of Archie and Olivia Manning's three sons. He was born in New Orleans, Louisiana, on March 24, 1976.

Peyton Manning has developed into one of the elite quarterbacks in NFL history.

Archie Manning took his sons to the NFL Pro Bowl in Hawaii in 1980. Making the trip was quite a thrill for four-year-old Peyton. He became friends with Walter Payton, the famous Chicago Bears running back. Payton sneaked away with the young boy for a boat ride.

Peyton had an older brother named Cooper and a younger brother named Eli. The Manning boys were close growing up. Peyton felt thankful that he had an older brother to look up to and a younger brother to protect. The boys played baseball, basketball, and football. All three were known as star athletes who had a famous dad.

Playing sports was an important part of life in the Manning household. But Archie never put pressure on his sons to be stars. He just wanted them to enjoy playing and to compete to the best of their abilities.

When Peyton was a young boy, Archie was the quarterback for the hometown New Orleans Saints. Archie was known as a very good player on a very bad team. He worked hard. He was determined to improve himself and his team. Peyton enjoyed watching his dad play football. But he didn't plan to follow in his father's footsteps and become an NFL quarterback.

Peyton's dad, Archie Manning, was a star quarterback for the New Orleans Saints.

Peyton learned from his father's example, though. He watched how his dad acted around fans. He noticed how Archie always treated them with respect. Peyton would remember this throughout his life.

Archie was well known around the United States. But he and Olivia made sure their boys had a normal home life. Meal time was always family time. The Mannings sat down together every morning at breakfast. Then the boys were off to school.

From left, Cooper, Archie, Peyton, and Eli Manning remain close as adults. They sometimes host football clinics together.

Peyton was an excellent student. But earning good grades didn't come easily to him. He studied hard. Sometimes, he even got up at 5:00 a.m. to do homework. Peyton developed a strong work ethic that would make him a successful student and athlete.

Peyton went to Isidore Newman High School in New Orleans. He was the star of the football team. He led the

All three Manning boys were star athletes in high school. A spinal condition prevented Cooper from playing football at the University of Mississippi. But Eli went on to play at Mississippi and later won a Super Bowl with the NFL's New York Giants.

team to a 34–5 record during his three years as the starting quarterback. Peyton improved as a player throughout high school. Every year, he completed more passes and threw more touchdowns. He was twice chosen as the Louisiana Class 2A Most Valuable Player (MVP).

In Peyton's senior year of high school, he was known more for his own talents than for having a famous father. He was named Gatorade Circle of Champions National Player of the Year after his last season at Isidore Newman. His talents also earned him an athletic scholarship to play football for the University of Tennessee.

Archie often reminded Peyton that he had to work harder as the competition grew stronger. Peyton's work ethic would be tested when he started college in Tennessee.

Peyton Manning

CHAPTER 2

FROM COLLEGE TO THE NFL

Fans of the Tennessee Volunteers football team were excited when Peyton Manning arrived on campus. They were certain he would be a future NFL star. But Manning wasn't all that certain of his future.

Manning worried about several things. He thought about his brother Cooper. Cooper's chance at playing pro football was destroyed by having a spinal injury. Manning also realized that only the most

Manning set many school passing records while playing for the Tennessee Volunteers.

At Tennessee, Manning always played his best in the most important games. One example was in the Citrus Bowl at the end of his junior season. Tennessee played Northwestern University. Manning won MVP honors in his team's 48–28 victory. He threw for 408 yards and four touchdowns.

talented, hardest working, and sometimes luckiest players ever reached the NFL. The young quarterback hoped to be one of the players who made it. But he worked hard in the classroom in case his dream didn't come true. He also knew that a pro football career didn't last very long. Having a good education would be important later in life. Manning did so well in his studies that he was named Phi Beta Kappa. That honor is given only to the finest students. By his junior year, he had already earned enough credits to graduate.

Manning was also becoming the best quarterback in college football. He became Tennessee's starting quarterback during his freshman year. As a sophomore, he turned into a star. He threw for 22 touchdowns and only four interceptions. In his final three years at Tennessee, Manning completed 63 percent

Manning was a popular player at Tennessee as he guided his team to four winning seasons.

of his passes. He also averaged 3,300 yards and 26 touchdowns per season.

Players are allowed to enter the NFL Draft after three years in college. Manning thought about entering the draft after his junior year. It was almost certain he would be picked first. But he chose to return to Tennessee for his senior year. Manning admitted that this was probably the toughest decision he ever

The Indianapolis Colts selected Manning with the first pick in the 1998 NFL Draft.

had to make. If he got hurt playing in college, he might never get to play in the NFL. But he decided to stay in school.

As a senior, Manning set school records for completed passes (287), passing yards (3,819), and touchdowns (36). He also won the Sullivan Award. It's given each year to the nation's top amateur athlete based on character and leadership abilities, as well as athletic achievement.

Manning had set 33 school records at Tennessee by the time he graduated. He had also set a Southeastern Conference record by passing for 300 or more yards in 18 separate games.

Manning grew up in a strong, loving family and had many opportunities to be successful. He decided to help less fortunate children be successful by establishing the PeyBack Foundation in 1999. This charity supports programs that give disadvantaged children opportunities for leadership and growth.

At Tennessee, Manning was used to being the star on a winning team. But that would soon change. The Indianapolis Colts selected him with the first pick in the 1998 NFL Draft. The Colts were a losing team. They hoped Manning would come in and turn things around.

Manning played well at times in his first season as an NFL quarterback. However, he also led the league in interceptions with 28. The Colts finished with a 3–13 record.

Having a losing record was tough for Manning to handle. But then he remembered the things he had learned from his father. Archie had always told Peyton that he would have to work harder as the competition got more difficult.

Peyton Manning

CHAPTER 3

BECOMING A STAR

The Colts hoped Peyton Manning would help reverse the team's losing history. However, they never could have imagined how quickly he would do it. The Colts improved from 3–13 in Manning's first season to 13–3 in his second year.

Manning's number of interceptions dropped from 28 to 15. He also racked up 26 touchdown passes and 4,135 passing yards. His success earned him a spot on the American Football Conference (AFC)

Manning was named to his first AFC Pro Bowl team after a stellar second season in 1999.

In 2000, Manning started the PeyBack Classic. It lets students from area high school football teams play at the Colts' home stadium. In 2003, Manning also launched the PeyBack Bowl. This football game features national and local celebrities in Indianapolis. The event raised more than $1.7 million in its first six years.

Pro Bowl team. The Colts were thrilled by how much Manning had improved. They were even more excited to be back in the playoffs for the first time in three years.

The playoffs did not go as expected, however. The Tennessee Titans upset the Colts at their home stadium in Indianapolis. Many fans blamed Manning for the Colts' loss. It would be the first of many playoff disappointments in his early pro career.

Manning continued to guide the Colts to victory in the regular season. He racked up amazing numbers over the next few years. In 2000, he led the NFL with 4,413 yards passing and 33 touchdowns. In 2001 and 2002, he averaged more than 4,100 yards and 26 touchdowns a year. Then in 2003, he had the best season of his career. He led the NFL by completing 67 percent of his passes and throwing for 4,267 yards.

Manning, *left,* **guided the Colts to a 12–4 record in 2004, but the team again fell short of a Super Bowl.**

Manning also won his first playoff games in 2003. The Colts scored a combined 79 points in beating the Denver Broncos and the Kansas City Chiefs. But the Colts lost to the powerful New England Patriots in the championship game of the AFC. Their season ended one game short of the Super Bowl.

In 2004, Manning had even more amazing numbers. He improved on the last season by completing 67.6 percent of his

Like his father did in the 1970s, Manning often takes time out to sign autographs for his fans.

passes. He also shattered the all-time NFL record by passing for 49 touchdowns. And in doing so, he tied a personal record by throwing only 10 interceptions. Some fans believed Manning had the best year ever by a quarterback. But in the playoffs, he struggled in another loss to the Patriots.

Manning won the NFL's MVP Award in both 2003 and 2004. But some players, coaches, and fans wondered if he was

In 2002, the PeyBack Foundation began a program that made it possible for 50 disadvantaged children to attend every Colts home game.

tough and determined enough to lead his team to the Super Bowl. Manning didn't let this criticism bother him. He knew that preparing well and playing to the best of his ability were all that he could do.

Manning also continued to help disadvantaged children through his PeyBack Foundation. The foundation set up programs that involved children in football. Manning and his charity also helped in other ways. In 2003, Manning created the Peyton's Pals program. It provides recreational and educational trips to 20 middle school students every month. Students have traveled to Washington DC and taken Disney cruises.

Manning and his Colts were eager to take a trip to the Super Bowl. Their fans were getting quite impatient, too.

Peyton Manning

CHAPTER 4

A SUPER BOWL CHAMPION

P eople continued to wonder if Peyton Manning could lead the Colts to the Super Bowl. Some thought he was too easygoing and willing to accept defeat. They thought this because Manning never showed much emotion on the field. He believed that he might lose his focus and concentration if he got caught up in his emotions.

Still, many people believed that Manning lacked the drive to lead his team to the championship.

Manning and the Colts had another strong regular season in 2005.

The performance of a quarterback is rated using a complex formula. It includes touchdown passes, interceptions, and completion percentage. In 2004, Manning scored a rating of 121.1. That was the highest rating in the history of the NFL. His overall career rating of 95.2 is the fifth best ever recorded.

He spent much of his career trying to prove them wrong. In fact, Manning and the Colts offense often scored lots of points. But the defense often gave up lots of points just as quickly. That changed in 2005.

The Colts had a strong offense and defense that year. The team went 14–2. They seemed headed for the Super Bowl. But once again, the Colts stumbled in the playoffs. They scored just three points in the first three quarters of the game they lost to the Pittsburgh Steelers.

This defeat left Manning terribly disappointed, but he didn't give up. In 2006, he led the Colts to a 12–4 record and the AFC Championship Game. That game was against the New England Patriots. The Patriots took an 18-point lead. Then Manning led an amazing rally. He guided his team downfield for the winning touchdown. Just one minute was left in the game!

Manning proved his critics wrong when he led the Colts to victory over the Chicago Bears in Super Bowl XLI.

The Colts beat the Patriots 38–34. The team was headed to its first Super Bowl since 1970.

 The Indianapolis Colts faced the Chicago Bears in Super Bowl XLI. The Colts beat the Bears 29–17. Manning threw for 247 yards and a touchdown. He was chosen as the game's MVP. But he refused to take credit for the win. Instead, he spoke about how the victory was won through a team effort.

Peyton and Eli Manning faced each other at the Pro Bowl following the 2008 season.

Manning was developing into one of the NFL's all-time best quarterbacks. He was also continuing to help others through his PeyBack Foundation. In 2004, the foundation set up the True Heroes program at St. Vincent Hospital in Indianapolis. The program holds a special event each month for children at the hospital. To honor Manning, the hospital was renamed Peyton Manning Children's Hospital at St. Vincent in 2007.

Manning's generosity has also been honored in other ways. Over the years, he has received many awards for his charity work. For example, he received the Henry P. Iba Citizen Award in 2002. That award is presented annually to individuals who excel in both athletics and charity work.

Manning also continued to win on the football field. From 2007 to 2009, he led the Colts to 13-, 12-, and 14-win seasons. He passed for more than 4,000 yards in each season. He also won the NFL MVP Award in 2008 and 2009.

In 2005, Hurricane Katrina destroyed much of the city of New Orleans. Peyton and Eli Manning sent a plane filled with relief supplies to their hometown. They wanted to help with the recovery effort.

In 2009, Manning guided the Colts to Super Bowl XLIV. They faced the New Orleans Saints, his father's old team. Manning performed well. He threw for 333 yards and a touchdown. But a key interception with three minutes remaining sealed the game. The Colts lost 31–17.

The Manning brothers' teams played each other twice through the 2010 season. Both times, Peyton Manning's Colts beat Eli Manning's New York Giants. The Colts defeated the Giants 26–21 in 2006 and 38–14 in 2010.

Manning was disappointed by the defeat. But he knew that he had prepared as well and played as hard as he could have. And that's all he ever asked of himself. He knew that if his family was proud of him, he could be proud, as well.

Hard work and passion for the game have helped Manning become one of the elite quarterbacks in NFL history. With his work ethic on the field and caring heart off of it, Manning figures to remain a superstar for a very long time.

Manning is expected to remain one of the top NFL quarterbacks for years to come.

FUN FACTS AND QUOTES

- When Peyton Manning was growing up, his father often gave him motivational quotes that he had clipped out of the newspaper. Manning credits one quote from Chuck Noll for helping him handle the pressure of being a quarterback. Noll was coach of the Pittsburgh Steelers from 1969 to 1991. He said, "Pressure is something that you feel only when you don't know what you're doing." These words inspired Manning to always be prepared.

- In 2001, Manning married college sweetheart Ashley Thompson. The couple lives in Indianapolis. But they stay in close contact with friends and family in Louisiana, Mississippi, and Tennessee.

- Few athletes are in more television commercials than Manning. He also hosted the popular late-night comedy program *Saturday Night Live* in 2007.

- When Manning was in junior high, one of his teachers encouraged him to try an activity outside sports. He chose acting. In one role, he played a Spanish dancer. He performed the tango wearing black pants, a yellow shirt, and a red sash around his waist! Archie still has the video of Peyton dancing.

WEB LINKS

To learn more about Peyton Manning, visit ABDO Publishing Company online at **www.abdopublishing.com**. Web sites about Manning are featured on our Book Links page. These links are routinely monitored and updated to provide the most current information available.

GLOSSARY

amateur
In sports, an athlete who isn't being paid for his or her work.

charity
Money given or work done to help people in need.

defense
The players on a football team who try to stop the other team's offense from scoring.

disadvantaged
In a worse position than others.

interception
In football, a pass thrown to a teammate but caught by someone on the opposing team.

offense
The players on a football team who control the ball and try to score points.

playoffs
A series of games played after the regular season to determine which teams should go on to the Super Bowl.

quarterback
In football, the player who directs the team's offensive play.

rally
A comeback.

scholarship
Money for tuition and other expenses given to a student by a college or other organization; often given to an outstanding athlete.

INDEX

FURTHER RESOURCES

MacCambridge, Michael. *America's Game: The Epic Story of How Pro Football Captured a Nation*. New York: Random House, 2004.

Manning, Peyton, Eli Manning, and Archie Manning. *Family Huddle*. Illus. Jim Madsen. N.p.: Scholastic Press, 2009.

Richards, Phil, and Mike Chappel. *Tales from the Indianapolis Colts Sidelines*. Champaign, IL: Sports Publishing LLC., 2004.